WITHDRAWN

MAY 02 2011

W9-BPK-714

WITHDRAWN

MAY 02 2011

WARREN-NEWPORT

WARREN NEWPORT
PUBLIC LIBRARY
224 N. O PLAINE RD
GURNEE, IL 60031

How does my Garden Grow?

DK Publishing

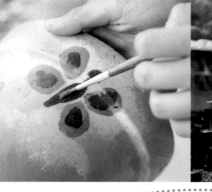

DK

LONDON, NEW YORK,
MELBOURNE, MUNICH, and DELHI

Senior designer Sonia Whillock-Moore
Senior editor Penny Smith
Additional design Rosie Levine, Rachael Grady,
Sadie Thomas, Lauren Rosier
Additional editing Wendy Horobin,
Lee Wilson, Lorrie Mack, Holly Beaumont
US editor Margaret Parrish
Photographer Will Heap
Additional photography Craig Robertson
Food stylist Denise Smart
Picture researcher Rob Nunn
RHS consultant Simon Maughan

Category publisher Mary Ling
Production editor Sean Daly
Production controller Claire Pearson
Jacket designer Sonia Whillock-Moore
Jacket editor Matilda Gollon

First published in the United States in 2011
by DK Publishing
375 Hudson Street, New York, New York 10014

Copyright © 2011 Dorling Kindersley Limited
Secret Seed characters copyright © 2011 Secret Seed Publications Limited

11 12 13 14 15 10 9 8 7 6 5 4 3 2 1
176266—December 2010

All rights reserved under International and Pan-American Copyright
Conventions. No part of this publication may be reproduced, stored in
a retrieval system, or transmitted in any form or by any means,
electronic, mechanical, photocopying, recording, or otherwise, without
the prior written permission of the copyright owner. Published in
Great Britain by Dorling Kindersley Limited.

A catalog record for this book
is available from the Library of Congress.
ISBN 978-0-7566-7194-5
Color reproduction by MDP, UK
Printed and bound by Toppan, China

Discover more at
www.dk.com

Contents

No garden? No problem!

Don't forget that **everything** in this book can be grown in a **box** or a **pot** or a **bag** or even a **sack**. Even the smallest **patio**, **balcony**, or **windowsill** can become a great garden.

Welcome to How Does My Garden Grow!

Keep your eyes open! Can you find these characters on the pages? See what they have to say.

Teeny tiny tomatoes   Mr. Corn   Mr. Rhubarb   Mrs. Basil   Miss Borage   Mr. Loofah   Mr. Pote

Guide to symbols

Throughout this book, you'll find an at-a-glance guide to keeping your plant healthy.

Does your plant like sun or shade? Find out here.

How much water does it need?

How long the plant takes to grow and other timely advice is here.

Important stuff

Grow peppers in a sunny, sheltered place.

Peppers need lots of moisture, so water them regularly.

Seeds usually take between 2 to 4 weeks to germinate.

Watch out!

All the growing, making, and cooking projects in this book are to be done under adult supervision. However, when this symbol appears, extra care should be taken.

Miss Carrot   Mr. Ivy   Mr. Pepper   Dragonfly   Calendula Boy   Mrs. Lavender   Mr. Wheat

What is a plant?

A plant is a living thing that feeds, grows, and produces new plants. There are nearly 400,000 different types of plant. They all have the same basic parts—leaves, stems, flowers, and roots.

Terminal bud
The main growing point of the plant.

Bees
and other insects help pollinate flowers.

Leaves

The leaves are where the plant captures energy from sunlight and uses it to turn nutrients into food. They are covered in tiny openings that let gases and moisture in and out of the plant.

Flowers

Many plants reproduce using flowers. Once the flowers have been fertilized, they produce seeds or fruit. Most nonflowering plants use their leaves, stems, or roots to make new plants.

Fruit

Stem

Stems support the leaves and flowers. They act as a transportation network to take water, minerals, and food to all parts of the plant. They have growing points along their length that produce leaves and new shoots.

Roots

Roots anchor the plant to its surroundings. They also suck up water and nutrients that the plant needs to grow. Sometimes roots are used to store food and water.

Root hairs
These take up most of the water from the soil.

Root tip
This is the part of the root that grows.

How do plants grow?

Seed leaf

True leaf

Here we go!

Most flowering plants begin life as a seed. Seeds are little packages that contain everything a new plant needs to grow—the baby plant itself and food to get it started.

Seeds will only start to grow when the conditions are right. The seed takes in water, which makes it swell and split the seed case. The main root emerges and reaches down into the soil.

The seed then sends up one or two tiny leaves. These are called cotyledons, or seed leaves. These are quickly followed by the first true leaves. The seedling can now begin to make its own food.

Flowers—the inside story

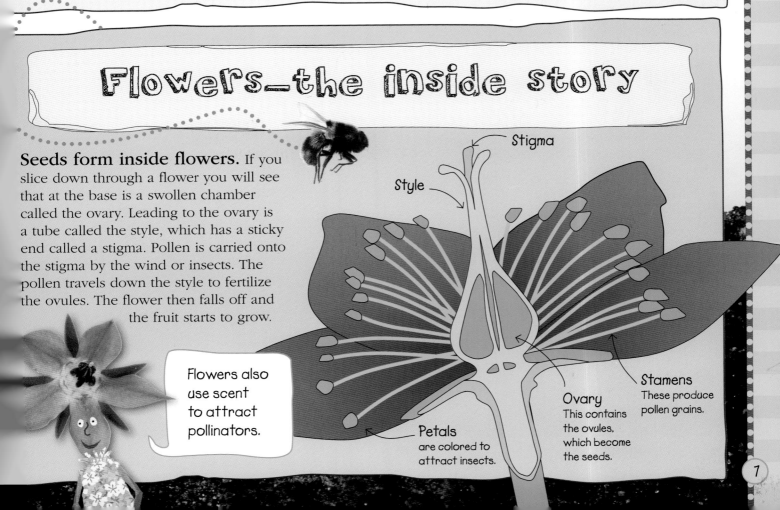

Seeds form inside flowers. If you slice down through a flower you will see that at the base is a swollen chamber called the ovary. Leading to the ovary is a tube called the style, which has a sticky end called a stigma. Pollen is carried onto the stigma by the wind or insects. The pollen travels down the style to fertilize the ovules. The flower then falls off and the fruit starts to grow.

Flowers also use scent to attract pollinators.

Stigma

Style

Stamens
These produce pollen grains.

Ovary
This contains the ovules, which become the seeds.

Petals
are colored to attract insects.

7

What plants need

Wild plants adapt to their environments—some like hot, dry weather; some like lots of rain; some like sandy soil. Garden plants also like particular conditions, so whenever you buy a plant from a garden center, or grow one from seed, make sure you give it what it needs to thrive.

Seeds

Soil

Soil is vital to plants—it anchors their roots and acts as storage for water and nutrients. Not all soils are the same, so gardeners often add compost made from dead plant material (like you'd find on a compost heap) to their soil to improve it.

You can also buy potting compost for growing plants in pots. It is usually a mix of soil, peat, sand, and nutrients. The ingredients vary according to what it's to be used for.

Check the labels

Read labels and seed packets when you buy plants and seeds. These tell you:

- What the plant looks like
- When to sow
- How to sow
- When to plant out in the garden
- When to harvest
- If the plant likes sun or shade
- The type of soil it prefers

The front of the seed packet shows the variety of the plant and what it will look like when fully grown.

- Grape-sized fruit in bunches
- Ideal for hanging baskets

☐ Sow   ☐ Plant out   ☐ Harvest

Spring	Summer	Autumn	Winter

Sowing and growing

- Sow indoors in early spring
- Sow seeds 6 mm (¼ in) deep in free-draining seed compost
- Plant outdoors in late spring or early summer
- Harvest late summer to autumn
- Likes full sun
- Prefers warm, well-drained soil

HEALTHY EATING High in vitamins A and E. Boosts the immune system.

Seed compost

A fine-textured mix that holds water well. It is low in nutrients because seeds already have their own store of food.

All-purpose compost

Most plants in this book will grow well in all-purpose compost.

Grow-bag compost

This is a nutrient-rich mixture specially prepared for hungry vegetables, such as bell peppers.

Sunlight

Like people, plants need energy to grow and reproduce. But unlike people, plants make their own food through a process called photosynthesis. To do this, plants take in carbon dioxide gas (CO_2) from the air and water from the soil, then use sunlight to convert them into glucose (a type of sugar). The plants then release waste oxygen gas (O_2) into the air.

Carbon dioxide + water + sunlight = glucose + oxygen

CO_2

O_2

Water

Water

Without water, plants wilt and die. However, most plants don't like waterlogged roots, so make holes in the bottom of the container and add broken pot or small stones to help the water drain. Always water plants before and after you plant them in a new pot.

Broken pot

Water carefully!

Peat-based compost

Carnivorous plants, such as sundews, need peat-based compost. Sometimes coir (coconut) fiber is used instead of peat.

Aquatic soil

This contains a slow-release fertilizer that does not leak into the water. This helps prevent algae and weeds from growing in the pond. Ordinary garden soil can also be used.

Mulch

Mulches are used to cover soil and help keep it moist. They also stop weeds from growing. Typical mulches include small stones, shells, straw, or wood chips.

Why we need plants

Without plants, we would not be able to live. They come into every area of our lives, from the air that we breathe, to the food we eat and the clothes we wear.

Food

The food we eat comes from plants. We eat...

roots (carrots and potatoes)

seeds (wheat)

leaves (herbs)

fruit (peppers and tomatoes)

stems (rhubarb)

Clothes

One of the most worn fabrics—cotton—comes from the seed pod of a cotton plant. This is spun into thread, then knitted into a fabric, and cut and stitched to make clothes.

Fuel

Coal, oil, and gas are made from plants that died millions of years ago and were squashed under the ground until they changed into what we call fossil fuel.

Paper

This is usually made from trees. The trees are cut down, then their lumber is mashed to pulp and flattened and dried.

Animals

These also eat plants, then we get food from them:
milk
meat
and eggs

Rope

This can be made from plant fibers such as Manila hemp. This type of rope was used to rig old sailing ships and is still made today.

Rubber boots

Latex is the milky sap of a rubber tree. It is used to make car tires, bouncy balls, and rain boots.

Latex drips into a bucket.

Housing

Thatch, a traditional roofing material, is often made from thick layers of straw or reed. This is tied to a house to make it watertight. In Ethiopia, the Dorze people use leaves from the false banana plant to thatch their houses.

Science stuff

People breathe in oxygen

People breathe out carbon dioxide

O_2

CO_2

Breathing

We breathe in air, which contains a gas called oxygen (O_2). We need oxygen to keep us alive. We breathe out a gas called carbon dioxide (CO_2). Plants take in carbon dioxide and give out oxygen.

O_2

CO_2

Plants give out oxygen

Plants take in carbon dioxide

flower from the cinchona tree

Medicine

Many medicines are made from plants, from creams for cuts and scratches to drugs that fight more serious illnesses. People with malaria suffer from headaches and fevers. Malaria can be treated by a drug called quinine, which comes from the bark of the South American cinchona tree.

Making stuff with things you've grown

Painting pots

Decorate your plastic or terra-cotta pots using acrylic paint, colored markers, and glitter. Just make sure you give your pots time to dry before you fill them with compost and plants.

You will nee
- metallic markers
- acrylic paint
- paintbrush
- craft glue
- glitter
- paper shapes
- clear craft varnish

Layer-painting a pot

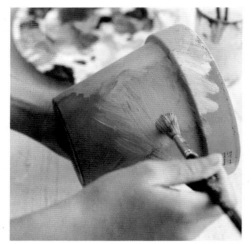

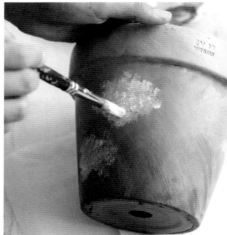

1 **This method** is for a multilayered picture. Brush a dark color on the base of the pot and lighter shades toward the top.

2 **Wait for the first coat** to dry, then add another color. We've dabbed on thick paint, straight from the tube, to make clouds.

3 **Add another layer** of paint when the second is d We have put butterflies on our po but you can add flowers, bugs, o whatever else you like!

Quick polka-dot pot

1 **Stick paper shapes** on your pot. We've used circles, but you can try stars or squares.

2 **Now paint over** the pot and paper circles with acrylic paint. Let it dry.

3 **Peel off** the circles to rev your pattern. Either leave it or paint the circles in different col

'se a silver metallic marker to make a magical night scene on a dark plastic pot.

Add a touch of luxury to a night-time stroll scene using a **golden metallic marker.**

Try mixing **metallic markers** and **acrylic paint** to make a fiery pot for hot crops.

Paint bands of glue on your pot. Sprinkle them with **glitter.** Then repeat with another glittery color.

Use the layer-painting techniques and make up your own designs.

for Mom

4 **Turn your pot** into a present by adding a name.

Hello!

Don't forget to varnish your paint and glitter pots to make them **weatherproof** and **long-lasting.**

 The finished pot—it hits the spot!

Plant labels

Help yourself remember what you planted—
and brighten up your garden—with jazzy plant
labels. Here are ideas for things to try,
but you can also make up your own
designs using recycled odds
and ends from home.

Use old **buttons**
to decorate
your labels.

Flower power

Use an old **CD, plastic milk
carton, pipe cleaner,** and
buttons to make this
dazzling label. Its shiny
surface will also scare
birds away. Glue everything
together with a quick-
setting, waterproof glue.

1. Start by cutting petal shapes out
of the plastic carton. Glue them to
the back of the CD, overlapping
them slightly.

2. Turn the CD over and
decorate with buttons and
a pipe cleaner. Finish by
attaching the flower
to a bamboo stick.

Recycled **plastic spoons
and forks** make perfect
bodies and
spiked legs for
these garden
helpers.

Red lettuce

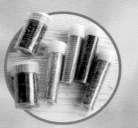

pe
eaners
ake good
gs and
ntennae.

Sprinkle on **glitter** to add
bling to your creations.

Plastic spoons and forks
make great bodies.

Cut up **plastic
cartons** to make
wings and things.
The plastic is soft
and strong.

Plastic straws
make bendy body
parts, such as
knees and elbows.

bubble-wrap
wings

plastic
yogurt
bottle

Garden helpers

Use washed pieces
of packaging, such
as **plastic cups**
and **foil food trays**,
to personalize
your helpers.

Lettuce

Sage

Corn

If you grow your own corn, you can pick it, cook it, and eat it right off the plant. This is when it is sweetest, since just a few hours after picking corn, its sugars turn to starch and the kernels lose some of their flavor. You can also buy corn seeds and grow corn for popcorn.

Science stuff

Corn is pollinated by the wind. The female flowers stay hidden in the leaves until the "silks" appear. The silks are long styles that hang out of the ear to catch pollen blown by the wind from another plant. The male flowers appear as a tassel at the top of the stem. Each pollinated silk becomes one kernel of corn.

You will need:

- corn seeds
- any potting compost
- small and large containers
- cardboard, old fabric, or plastic for lining container
- grow-bag compost
- tomato fertilizer
- bamboo poles (optional)

1 **Corn** is a type of cereal grass. Its seeds are the dried kernels of corn on the cob.

2 **Sow the seeds** about ½ in (1.5 cm) deep in any kind of potting compost. Water regularly and keep in a warm place until the seeds start to sprout. Seedlings start to appear in 7 to 21 days.

3 **Once the leaves** appear, start putting your plants outside in the sun for a few hours each day. Don't leave them outside until all risk of frost has gone.

4 **Corn** has long roots, so choose a large container (or plant directly in the ground). Cover any holes with cardboard, old fabric, or plastic bags with drainage holes.

5 **Plant** young plants in grow-bag compost, being careful not to disturb the roots. Plant in blocks to help pollination. Place your plants in full sun and keep them well watered.

6 **If roots appear** on the surface, cover them over with compost. Feed the plants with tomato fertilizer every two weeks.

male flower

female flower where fruit forms

7 **You may need** to support your plants with bamboo poles as they grow. The cobs are ready to test for ripeness when the silks turn brown.

silks

kernels

husk

Test the cobs for ripeness by pressing a thumbnail into a kernel. If a creamy liquid comes out, the cob is ready. If it's watery, leave it a bit longer.

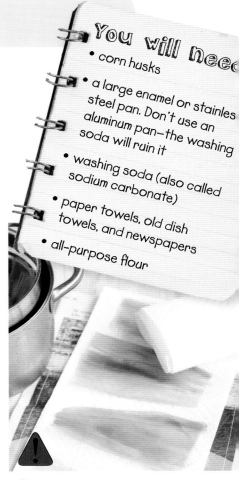

Make it

Corn paper

The leaves that are tightly wrapped around corn are called the husk. You can flatten these and paste them together to make paper. It takes about two weeks to dry, but then you can use it to make beautiful gifts.

You will need
- corn husks
- a large enamel or stainless steel pan. Don't use an aluminum pan—the washing soda will ruin it
- washing soda (also called sodium carbonate)
- paper towels, old dish towels, and newspapers
- all-purpose flour

Wear rubber gloves during steps 2 and 3.

1 **Cut the top** and bottom off the corncob and carefully peel off the husk. Try to keep each leaf in one piece. Make sure you have an adult helping you.

2 **Fill a large pan** with water and stir in 1 tbsp washing soda for every quart (liter) of water. Add the husks, bring to a boil, and simmer for about 30 minutes.

3 **Rinse the leaves** in plenty of cold water and leave them to drain on paper towels or an old dish towel. Pat them as dry as possible with paper towels.

To make flour paste, mix together 1 tsp flour and 2 tsp water.

The finished paper

4 **Arrange the leaves** in a row so the edges overlap slightly. Stick the edges together with flour paste.

5 **Spread the leaves** with paste, then put another layer on top at 90 degrees to the first. This is one sheet of paper.

6 **Sandwich** your paper between dish towels, then newspaper. Weight down with something heavy. Replace the newspaper when wet.

Paint someone special a mini masterpiece on the paper you've made. You will need a frame and some acrylic paints and brushes.

Make a gift tag

Make a notebook

Cover a notebook with brown postal wrapping paper and stick a piece of corn paper on top. Then paint a picture to decorate it.

Make a hole with a pen and thread some ribbon through each cover to finish the book.

Plants for a fragrant garden

A garden is not just pretty to look at—if you choose the right plants, it can surround you with sweet smells all year round. The perfume comes from oils stored in the flower's petals that are released as it opens.

Roses

Flowers produce **strong scents** to attract insects and birds to pollinate them. When flowers smell nice, animals know there is pollen and nectar inside. As they land on each bloom, pollen clings to their feet and bodies and they carry it to the next flower. But not all flowers smell sweet—some have a horrible scent to attract flies!

There are some plants that only open and release their scent at night. They do this to attract night-flying pollinators, such as moths and bats.

The classic **rose** fragrance is one of the best-loved scents. There are lots of different types of rose flower. They come in a range of colors, and some have petals that are particularly thick and velvety.

Freesia

Spring flower with a powerful scent.

Jasmine

Wonderful, delicately scented white blooms.

Honeysuckle

Brightly colored, with honey-scented flowers.

Orchid

Orchids range in smell from fruity to spicy.

Fragrant flower gallery

Honeysuckle

Nicotiana

Lavender

Nicotiana blooms—also known as **flowering tobacco**—open and release their powerful fragrance when the sun goes down. Nicotiana likes moist, fertile soil and is happiest growing in partial shade. Its flowers come in reds, pinks, whites, or greens.

Turn the page to find out how to grow your own lavender.

Honeysuckle is a strong climber that is easy to grow. The vine produces bright flowers during the summer. Plant it in the ground, then train it up a trellis.

Lavender is a classic scented flower. It is native to North Africa and the area around the Mediterranean sea, but is now loved all over the world.

Lavender

You can grow lavender from seeds, but it is especially easy to grow from a cutting taken from a healthy, full-grown plant. It's a good idea to take several cuttings at once, so you still end up with a new plant even if some of the cuttings don't root.

You will need:

- a mature lavender plant
- small pots
- seed compost
- a clear plastic bag and rubber bands to hold it in place
- a larger pot

2 **Carefully pull off** the leaves on the bottom half of the stem to leave a clean stalk.

1 **Choose a new** flower-free shoot on the parent plant. Pull it down and away from the main stem, making sure you include a bit of the heel (the older wood at the base of each shoot).

This is the "heel"

3 **Fill a pot** with seed compost, and make a hole in the middle. Plant the cutting in the hole, then water it.

5 **It takes** around six weeks for the cutting to develop its own roots. When it starts to produce new leaves, it is ready to plant in a bigger pot, where it will grow and flower.

4 **Keep the cutting** warm and moist. One way to do this is to cover it with a plastic bag. Make sure the bag doesn't touch the cutting.

Lavender roots rot if the soil is too wet, so don't overwater your plants.

24

Science stuff

Lavender is used as a herbal medicine to kill germs and help people relax. Its fragrance comes from an oily chemical in its flowers called linalool.

Fresh lavender

Dried lavender

Lavender oil

Lavender cream

Lavender buddy

You can dry bunches of lavender by hanging them in a warm, dark place. After a month, they'll be ready to stuff this odd little character. He's made from an old sock—but the lavender makes him smell sweet!

You will need:

- old sock
- uncooked rice
- dried lavender flowers
- needle and thread
- stick-on eyes
- scraps of fabric
- pipe cleaners

1 **Fill a sock** with a mixture of rice and dried lavender flowers. The rice adds weight and helps the lavender go a bit further.

2 **Twist the end** of the sock to keep the lavender and rice in place. Secure it with a few stitches.

4 **Draw arms** and legs on fabric and cut them out. For thicker limbs, fold the fabric in half and cut through both layers. Then stitch around the edges.

5 **Attach the arms** and legs securely to the body with a few firm stitches.

6 **Make curly hair** for your lavender buddy by wrapping pipe cleaners around a pencil.

I'm made from a sock, too! Cardboard in my tail keeps it stiff, and my fins are made of candy wrappers.

3 **Now stitch** on a mouth using brightly colored thread. Peel the backs off the eyes and stick them in place.

7 **Sew the middles** of the pipe cleaners to the top of his head and bend them to make a wild hairstyle.

Insect-eating plant

Here's a mini world in a jar, and the plant at the center is an insect-eating sundew. Place it on a sunny windowsill and ticky droplets form on its leaves. Passing insects stick to these and re digested to death. Team up the sundew with modeling clay liens to make a bottle garden that's out of this world!

Sundews like to live in a sunny spot.

Keep well watered. Sundews only drink soft water or rainwater.

Some sundews can live for up to 50 years.

You will need:

- aquarium gravel or recycled beads and stones
- large plastic storage jar
- glitter
- carnivorous-plant potting compost
- sundew carnivorous plant
- modeling clay

1 **Start by dropping** colored gravel into the bottom of your storage jar. Make layers using different colors and sprinkle on glitter for sparkle.

2 **Now drop in handfuls** of potting compost. Press it down gently. Make sure you leave enough room for the sundew!

4 **Make your alien.** No one knows what an alien looks like, so they can be any shape you like! Mold some modeling clay into a body and add eyes, arms, and legs

5 **Here's one we made** earlier. Think about where your alien will go. Inside the jar? Sticking to the outside? This will help you decide how big to make it

Plant watch

Sundews are also called Drosera. There are more than 160 types. They attract insects using their bright colors and the sweet droplets that cover their leaves. Once an insect is stuck, some Drosera curl their leaves around it as it dies.

3 **Remove the sundew** from its pot, plant it in the middle of the potting compost, and press the compost gently around it.

Small fly

6 **Leave your alien** world to settle. The sundew will start to form new droplets on its leaves that small flies will stick to.

Top tip

Carnivorous plants usually like a peat and sand mix of compost. You can buy it already mixed or make your own using two parts moss peat to one part sand.

Plants for topiary

Topiary is the centuries-old art of clipping trees and shrubs into decorative shapes. It's also a way of training climbing plants around a frame. The result is anything from a neat pom-pom to an elephant.

Making shapes

Use a small-leaved, evergreen plant. Since the leaves remain all year, so does your shape! You'll also need a wire frame to grow plants around or to use as a guide to cutting. Buy or make your frame.

A wire frame can be simple, like a heart, or more complicated, like this seahorse. Wrap the plant around the frame as it grows. Snip off any shoots growing in the wrong direction.

For clipped topiary, put your frame over the plant. Snip the plant to the shape of the frame.

Trim little and often as your plant takes shape.

Cone

Chicken

Pom-pom

Privet

raditionally used or garden hedges.

Yew

A dense, slow-growing evergreen.

Box

Good for small topiary.

Shrubby honeysuckle

A fast-growing hedging plant.

Juniper

A hardy plant with dense leaves.

Choose a healthy plant with an even shape

Plant watch

When you snip your plant, keep the cuts neat—ragged edges look untidy. Ideally, trim in early summer. Never trim when there is a frost, since this can damage the plant.

Topiarists trim their creations using scissors, pruning shears, or hand shears. Electric hedge trimmers can also be used for large creations.

Topiary shears

Spiral topiary

Elephant and rider

Important stuff

Ivy grows best out of direct sunlight keep in a sheltered place.

Water ivy when the soil begins to feel dry–but don't let it dry out.

The ivy should cover the frame in 2 to 3 months.

Ivy man

If you don't want to wait for years for a topiary figure to take shape, try your hand at this ivy man. He's made from a wire frame and will spring to life in just a few months.

You will need:

- garden wire
- scissors or wire cutters
- window box or similar container
- all-purpose potting compost
- small stick
- metal food tray
- two small-leaved ivy plants

1 **For the head,** ask an adult to help you twist a length of wire into an oval, leaving enough wire to make the neck. Make sure your ivy man is the right size to fit the container.

2 **Take another** length of wire and make a second oval, twisting it around the first to make a 3-D head. Secure it at the neck.

4 **Fill a container** with all-purpose potting compost. Position your ivy man. To help him stand up, try making a shovel from a stick and metal food tray. Plant the ivy.

5 **Plant ivy** at the base of each leg and wrap the tendrils around the frame.

Plant watch

Ivy is a climbing plant that loves to scramble up walls, trees, and fences. It can reach as high as 100 ft (30 m) above the ground. Ivy hauls itself up using aerial roots that grow along its stem. These help the plant to grip the surface.

Take your time making
your wire frame—
the more wire you use,
the stronger it will be.

⚠️

3 Make the body by
twisting more wire into a
body shape. Include spikes to anchor
the frame in the ground. Attach the
body to the head and wrap more
wire around the whole thing.

6 As the ivy grows, thread
it through the frame. Clip out
any shoots that are growing in the
wrong direction. After a few months,
they will cover the whole frame.

Grow a loofah

Loofahs usually grow in warm countries, but will grow in a sunny, sheltered spot in cooler climates, or in a greenhouse or solarium. They produce long, green fruit. When the fruit is young, you can cook and eat it in the same way as a zucchini.

1 **First, soak the seeds** in warm water for a couple of hours. Then plant them in individual pots of seed compost and cover with a light layer of compost.

2 **Cover your seeds** with a plastic bag until they germinate. Put them in a sunny spot and keep them well watered.

Loofahs grow quickest in hot climates. When it is cooler, they grow more slowly and produce fewer fruits.

3 **Loofah plants grow** quickly. When they have at least one pair of leaves, they are ready to plant in a bigger container.

Important stuff

Grow in a sunny, sheltered spot or in a greenhouse or solarium.

Loofahs need plenty of water and well-draining soil.

Seeds usually take 1 to 3 weeks to germinate.

4 **Loofahs** need lots of room for their roots, so choose a large container. Add some broken polystyrene packaging for drainage. This will make your container lighter and easier to move.

5 **Fill the container** with all-purpose compost and add a trellis for the plant to grow up. Either buy the trellis, or make your own using sticks and string.

Flowers start to appear about eight weeks after planting.

6 **Plant your loofah** in the large container. Thread it through the trellis as it grows. Feed your loofah plant with tomato fertilizer every couple of weeks.

7 **The fruit** grows at the base of the female flower. Some loofah plants can produce around 20 loofah fruits at a time.

Bath loofah

If you leave your loofah on the vine until it turns brown, you can use it to make a back sponge for the bath. The part you need is the network of fibers just under the skin.

The plant used the fibers to transport water when it was alive.

You will need:
- loofah
- household bleach
- pair of scissors
- length of ribbon
- gift box or bag
- bath items, such as soap or a washcloth

1 **Pick your loofah** when it is fully grown, dry, and beginning to shrivel. You should be able to hear the seeds rattle when you shake it.

2 **Cut off** the blossom end of the loofah and shake out the seeds. Leave them to dry, then you can try growing new loofahs from them the following year.

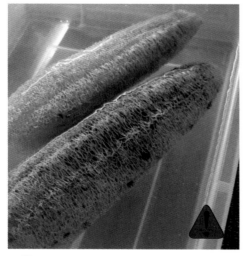

3 **Crack the loofah skin** and peel it off. If it's a bit tough, soak the loofah in warm water first to soften the skin.

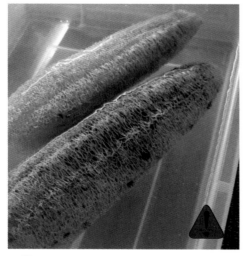

4 **Soak the loofah** in a bucket of water mixed with 1 tbsp bleach. This should kill off any mold spores.

5 **Rinse well** in clean water and let it dry. Cut your loofah to a useful size with a pair of scissors.

6 **Make a hole** near one end of the loofah and thread a piece of ribbon through to make a loop. You can then hang it up in the bathroom.

Make a pamper gift set

Put your loofah in a gift box or bag with scented soap and a washcloth. It's a perfect pamper present!

Plants for a container pond

Aquatic plants are specially adapted to a watery environment and are vital ingredients for a pond. They provide oxygen, shade, shelter, and food for fish and other water creatures.

These plants provide useful resting places for dragonflies and their flowers are attractive to bees.

Emerging:
Sweet flag
(*Acorus calamus*)

Emerging:
Umbrella plant
(*Cyperus alternifolius*)

Emerging:
Duck potato
(*Sagittaria latifolia*)

Marginal:
Greater spearwort
(*Ranunculus lingua*)

Emerging plants have roots in shallow water

Giant water lilies

Giant water lilies are truly enormous! Their leaves can grow up to 10 ft (3 m) across. They have white flowers that open at night and give out a scent to attract beetles. At daybreak, the flower closes, trapping the beetles, which become covered in pollen. The beetles are released later that evening, and move on to pollinate a new flower. The flower then turns pink.

Oxygenating plants provide oxygen for underwater creatures like fish.

These plants provide shade for the pond.

Floating plants
have leaves that float on the surface

Oxygenating: Hornwort (*Ceratophyllum demersum*)

Marginal: Bog primula (*Primula florindae*)

Marginal: Marsh marigold (*Caltha palustris*)

Floating: Frogbit (*Hydrocharis morsus-ranae*)

Floating: Water soldier (*Stratiotes aloides*)

Marginal plants
like to live in wet, boggy soil

Oxygenating plants
live underwater

Container pond

This mini pond will fit on a patio or balcony. Put it in a shady place where it won't dry out, and set it up in its final position so you don't have to drag it when it's full of water.

You will need:

- clean bricks and gravel
- large 10 gallon (40 liter) container for water
- aquatic plants
- plastic basket and burlap
- fish (optional)
- rainwater

Don't put too many plants in your pond—leave room for the fish!

1 **Arrange clean bricks** in the bottom of the container to make platforms for the plants. Put clean gravel in the bottom, then fill two-thirds full with rainwater.

2 **Put the oxygenating** plants, such as this hornwort, in first. Check the plant labels, since some types need to be anchored in the gravel, while others float freely in the water.

3 **Marginal plants**, such as sweet flag, go in next. Leave these in their pots, but put a layer of gravel on the soil to help keep it in place. Place the pots on the bricks at the edge of the pond.

4 **You can group** marginal plants like marsh marigold and bog primula together. Line a plastic basket with burlap, fill with soil, then plant your plants. Finish with a layer of gravel.

5 **Fill the container** to the top with water. Then carefully place one or two floating plants on the surface. Make sure that some of the water surface is left clear of plants.

6 **Now add your fish!** Small goldfish or mosquito fish are perfect for mini ponds. They feed on mosquito larvae and algae. Move fish to a larger container as they grow.

Put a stick in your pond as an escape route for small creatures that fall in!

Carefully add your fish to the pond so you don't injure them. Lower the bag all the way into the water and let the fish swim out.

Top tip
Fill or top off your pond with rainwater, since tap water often has chlorine in it, which can kill fish. If you have to use tap water, let it stand for a few days so the chlorine evaporates—then add your fish.

Growing things and cooking

Growing herbs

Here we grow oregano, parsley, and thyme from seed. We also show how to separate out a pot of supermarket basil. Like the other herbs here, basil can easily be grown from seed. However, in winter it's best to grow it on a sunny windowsill from herbs grown in pots.

Herbs are ideal for growing in containers. Just keep us in shape by regularly using our stems and leaves in cooking.

1 **Collect a number** of fruit juice cartons. These will make colorful containers for your herbs. They also have a waterproof lining and will not fall apart.

2 **Cut off the top quarter** of the carton using scissors. Then make drainage holes in the bottom using a pen or pencil.

3 **Join your containers** together with large paper clips. Arrange them in a pattern—they look better if you put any writing to the back.

4 **Put a few stones** at the bottom of each carton for drainage, then fill them with all-purpose compost. It may be easier to do this if you make a cone out of paper or cardboard.

5 **Sprinkle a few** oregano, parsley, and thyme seeds into separate cartons. Cover with a thin layer of compost, water, and leave in a well-lit place to germinate. Keep the herbs lightly watered.

6 **Thin out** the seedlings if they get crowded. You can eat the little plants you've pulled out. Don't let your herbs dry out.

Potted herbs

1 **Supermarket** potted basil, like other potted herbs, is really lots of little plants growing closely together. To separate these, gently tease the roots apart with a pencil. This is called "pricking out."

2 **Gently transfer** each plant to a new container. Press the compost around the plants, then water them. This method works for most herbs grown in containers.

Oregano

Parsley

Thyme

Important stuff

Herbs like to be in a warm, sunny place outdoors. Some shade is okay.

Water every other day to keep the soil damp.

Germination can take up to 28 days—check the package for each herb.

Herby cheese muffins

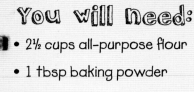

You will need:

- 2½ cups all-purpose flour
- 1 tbsp baking powder
- 1 tsp salt
- 1 tsp mustard powder
- 1 cup plus 1 tbsp grated sharp Cheddar cheese
- 2 tbsp chopped fresh parsley
- 1 tbsp chopped fresh oregano
- 2 tsp chopped fresh thyme
- freshly ground black pepper
- 2 eggs
- 7 fl oz (200 ml) lowfat milk
- 5 tbsp butter, melted

yummy

Here is a herby muffin recipe that uses parsley, oregano, and thyme. The muffins are irresistible and best eaten the day they're made, although they will la for a couple of days if you keep them in a container.

1 **Preheat the oven** to 375°F (190°C). Line a muffin pan with 10 paper baking cups. Then sift the flour, baking powder, and salt into a bowl.

2 **Add the mustard,** three-quarters of the cheese, and the parsley, oregano, and thyme. Season with black pepper and mix everything together.

3 **In another bowl,** beat together the eggs, milk, and melted butter, and pour over the dry ingredients.

4 **Stir the mixture** until everything is just combined. Your batter should be quite lumpy.

5 **Spoon the batter** into the baking cups, then sprinkle the rest of the cheese on top. Bake for 20–25 minutes, until risen and firm.

Basil and tomato muffins

To make these, simply follow the main recipe, but swap the herbs for 2 tbsp chopped fresh basil, and stir in ½ cup chopped sun-dried tomatoes.

Tiny tomatoes

Even when you are short of space, you can still grow an impressive pot of little tomatoes. The tomatoes shown here are a type called "100s and 1,000s," but there are lots of other varieties to choose from. Just check the seed package to make sure they are suitable for where you want to grow them.

Plant watch
Once the plants have several new leaves, they are ready to repot.

Important stuff

Tomatoes grow best in a sunny, sheltered place.

Water to keep the compost moist, but not soggy.

From planting seeds to picking tomatoes— about 4 months.

1 **Sprinkle** seeds onto seed compost. Cover with ¼ in (6 mm) more compost. Plant just a few more seeds than you think you'll need, since most should germinate.

2 **Keep the** seeds in a warm place. When the seedlings start to push through the compost, move the plants to a sunny position.

3 **You'll need** plenty of drainage holes in your large container. An adult can make these using a hammer and nail. Thick tape stops the nail from slipping.

4 **Fill the container** with all-purpose potting compost. Dig small holes and place two or three plants in the holes. Try not to disturb the roots.

5 **Press the compost** around the plants, making sure all the roots are covered.

6 **Put the plants** back in their sunny spot and keep them well watered as they grow.

Top tips

When tiny fruit begins to appear, feed the plant with tomato food to help it ripen. You can buy the food at garden centers.

When a fertilized flower dies back, a small green tomato forms in its place. This grows bigger and turns orange, then bright red when it's ripe. That's when it is good to eat! However, don't eat tomato leaves—they contain small amounts of a poisonous chemical.

Tomato pizza

Use your little tomatoes to make delicious fresh pizza. Simply sprinkle them whole over the top before you bake. Then when you take a bite, they burst in your mouth with a delicious, sweet tomato taste!

we're life-sized!

You will need:

- 2 cups strong white bread flour, plus extra for dusting
- ½ tsp salt
- ½ tsp instant dried yeast
- ⅔ cup warm water
- 1 tbsp extra-virgin olive oil, plus extra for greasing
- ⅔ cup passata (or tomato sauce)
- 1 tbsp tomato paste
- ½ tsp sugar
- 1 tbsp chopped fresh basil or oregano, plus extra to garnish
- 7 oz (200 g) mozzarella cheese, drained and sliced
- ½ cup grated Cheddar cheese
- 5 oz (125 g) tiny tomatoes

1 **For the base,** put the flour, salt, and yeast in a large mixing bowl. Make a well in the center and pour in the water and oil. Use a wooden spoon to mix the ingredients into a dough.

2 **Put the dough** on a lightly floured surface. Then knead it for 7–10 minutes, until it feels smooth and elastic.

3 **Place the dough** in a lightly oiled bowl and cover it with plastic wrap. Let it rise for about an hour, or until it has doubled in size.

4 **For the sauce,** put the passata (or tomato sauce), tomato paste, sugar, and chopped herbs in a small pan and simmer gently for 4–5 minutes. Let cool.

Cook it

Preheat the oven to 425°F (220°C). Bake the pizza for 10–12 minutes, or until it is crisp and golden. Sprinkle fresh herbs on top before serving.

5 **Use your fist** to press down the dough and punch out any air bubbles. Then knead it on a lightly floured surface. Next, roll out to make a 12 in (30 cm) circle.

6 **Place the dough** on a baking sheet, then top with the tomato sauce, mozzarella, grated Cheddar, and tiny tomatoes.

tiny tomatoes

Growing potatoes

Potatoes are easy, cheap, and lots of fun to grow. And everyone loves eating them—roasted, baked, mashed, or as fabulous fries or delicious, crunchy chips.

Important stuff

Put the plants in a light, airy place that is sheltered from frost.

Water regularly during flowering, but make sure not to overwater.

Plant in the spring and harvest in the summer.

Science stuff

A potato is a type of tuber. Tubers are swollen parts of a plant stem or root. The plant uses these to store nutrients during the winter so it can produce new shoots and roots in the spring. Potatoes are stem tubers, which form from underground stems called rhizomes. Sweet potatoes and yams are root tubers.

root tuber

stem tuber

1 **Place seed potatoes,** eye end up, in an empty egg carton. Leave them in a light, unheated place until they sprout.

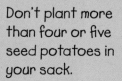
Don't plant more than four or five seed potatoes in your sack.

2 **Line a rolled-down sack** with a thick garbage bag. Make drainage holes in the bottom. Plant the potatoes in an all-purpose potting compost, with the shoots pointing up. Cover with more potting compost.

3 **When green stalks** and leaves grow, cover the stalks with more potting compost and partly roll up the sack. This allows more potatoes to grow off the stalks. It is called hilling up.

4 **Keep hilling up** as the plants grow, so you cover more and more of the stems. Unroll the bag and sack a little each time, until it is fully unrolled, leaving just the leaves.

5 **The potatoes** are ready for harvesting when the leaves begin to turn yellow. Cut the sack to get them out.

6 **Remove the potatoes** and leave them on the ground for a few hours to dry out.

Growing carrots

You can grow all kinds of carrots—large ones, round ones, and different-colored ones. The first wild carrots were purple, yellow, or white and tasted bitter but, over centuries, gardeners have bred all colors of carrot to be sweet and juicy.

Important stuff

Carrots like sun, so make sure they get some for at least part of the day.

Carrots need lots of moisture, so water them regularly.

Seeds usually take about 2 weeks to germinate.

Choose a deep container so there is plenty of room for the roots.

1 **You can grow carrots** in all kinds of containers. Here, we've used a burlap bag. It is lined with a trash bag, stapled in place. Remember to poke a few drainage holes in your container.

2 **Carrot seeds are small,** so you might want to mix them with a little sand so you can plant them evenly.

3 **Fill your container** to just below the top with an all-purpose potting compost. Make shallow trenches. Thinly sprinkle the seeds in the trenches and cover them over.

4 **You may need** to thin out your carrot plants as they push through the soil. You should leave a gap of roughly 2 in (5 cm) between each plant.

Top tip

Carrots keep for months if you trim off the leaves, then layer them in slightly damp sand, making sure they aren't touching. The sand should be 2–3 fingers deep between layers.

5 **Carrots** need plenty of water as they grow. This encourages good root growth and large, healthy carrots. Add an all-purpose liquid fertilizer once a week when the leaves start to grow rapidly.

Carrots provide our bodies with vitamin A. This is good for our eyes.

6 **When the carrots** are big enough to eat—this could be as soon as 12 weeks after planting—gently lift them from the soil. Wash them well, and then you can eat them!

Potato and carrot chips

Use your homegrown potatoes and carrots to make delicious oven-baked chips. Once you've made these, experiment with other vegetables, such as parsnips and red beets.

You will need:

For the potato chips
- 2 medium potatoes
- 2 tsp sunflower oil
- salt and pepper
- 1–2 tsp paprika (optional)

For the carrot chips
- 2 medium carrots
- 2 tsp sunflower oil
- 2 tsp honey
- salt and pepper

1 **For the potato chips,** preheat the oven to 350°F (180°C). Slice the potatoes using a vegetable peeler. Mix them with the oil, salt, pepper, and paprika, if using.

2 **Line a baking sheet** with parchment paper and arrange the potato slices in a single layer. Cook for 10 minutes, and turn them over. Cook 10 minutes more.

2 **Line a baking sheet** with parchment paper. Arrange the carrots in a single layer and cook for 10 minutes. Turn the chips over and cook for another 7–10 minutes.

1 **For the carrot chips,** preheat the oven to 350°F (180°C). Use a vegetable peeler to slice the carrots thinly. Mix them with the oil, honey, salt, and pepper.

57

Top tip

Keep your eye on the chips as they cook and remove them from the oven when they turn golden. Cool on a wire rack.

Bell peppers

The next time you buy bell peppers at the supermarket, don't throw away the seeds. Instead, plant them so they grow into new pepper plants. Choose fresh orange or red peppers for your seeds, since these are the most likely to grow.

Important stuff

Grow peppers in a sunny, sheltered place.

Peppers need lots of moisture, so water them regularly.

Seeds usually take between 2 to 4 weeks to germinate.

I'm a red pepper. This means I'm ripe! Most green peppers are just unripe red, orange, or yellow peppers.

You will need:

- ripe bell pepper
- spoon
- small pots
- seed compost
- large container
- grow-bag compost
- tomato fertilizer
- lots of water
- mulch

1 **Cut open** your pepper, then use the handle end of a spoon to push out the seeds. Be gentle, so you don't damage the seeds.

2 **Now, wash** the seeds in water. This gets rid of a natural antigerminating substance that stops the seeds from growing inside the fruit—or in your pot!

3 **Plant your seeds** about ¼ in (6 mm) deep in pots filled with seed compost. Make sure they have room for their roots to spread.

4 **When the plants** begin to fill their pots, plant them into larger containers of grow-bag compost. Feed with tomato fertilizer every two weeks.

5 **Peppers need** lots of moisture, so water them regularly. To keep the compost damp, try covering it with mulch, since this helps hold in moisture.

Plant watch

The bell peppers your plant produces may not look the same as the one you took the seeds from!

This is because many supermarket peppers are hybrids (plants whose parents were different varieties), so their offspring may take after one of the parents. Sometimes the seeds will not grow at all—but it's still fun to try!

Science stuff

Many plants have fruits that start off green and change color. This is the result of a chemical change in the green pigment, called chlorophyll.

As the fruit ripens, the chlorophyll breaks down into a series of different-colored chemicals. The change shows that the seeds are maturing. At the same time, the fruit becomes sweeter and softer.

Pepper hummus

Now that you've grown your bell peppers, it's time to eat them. So here's a recipe for red pepper hummus. If you have any spare peppers, use them to make delicious little serving dishes.

You will need:

- 2 red bell peppers
- $2/3$ cup canned chickpeas
- 1 tsp paprika
- 1 clove garlic, peeled
- juice of ½ lemon
- 1 tbsp tahini
- 3 tbsp olive oil
- salt and pepper
- bell pepper shells, to serve

1 Cut each pepper into four pieces and remove the stalks and seeds. Preheat the broiler to high.

2 Line a broiler pan with foil and place the peppers skin-side up. Broil for 5 minutes, or until the skins have blackened.

3 Put the hot peppers into a plastic bag and seal it up. When the bell peppers are cool enough to handle, peel off the blackened skins.

4 Put the bell peppers, chickpeas, paprika, garlic, lemon juice, tahini, and olive oil in a food processor and blend until smooth. Season to taste.

5 Spoon the hummus into the bell pepper shells and serve.

Take out my seeds before you use me as a pot.

Top tip

Serve the hummus with pita bread and carrot and cucumber strips. Don't forget to eat the bell pepper containers!

Edible flowers

Not all flowers are edible, but you can eat some, including the calendula and borage shown here. It is best to grow your own edible flowers, because then you know they are free from dangerous pesticides and other garden chemicals, and are safe to eat.

Important stuff

Planting instructions vary, so check your seed packages.

Water your plants regularly to prevent them from wilting.

Pick flowers in the cool of the morning after the dew has gone.

Growing calendula

Calendula flowers can be yellow to bright orange. They have a mildly peppery taste.

Only the petals of calendula flowers should be eaten.

1 **Sprinkle calendula** seeds over a pot of seed compost and cover with ¼ in (6 mm) more compost.

2 **Once the seedlings** start to emerge, plant them into an all-purpose compost in a larger pot. Water them regularly as they grow.

Growing borage

This pretty blue flower has a light cucumberlike flavor.

Only eat borage flowers—or use them as food decoration.

Watch out! Borage stems and leaves are covered in prickly hairs.

1 **Plant seeds** in seed compost and cover with more compost. Put the pots in a sunny, sheltered place. It should take about a week for the seeds to germinate.

2 **When the plants** start to fill the pots, choose the healthiest ones and plant in their final containers. Use all-purpose compost.

Pansies

Lavender

Elderflowers

Nasturtiums

Dandelions

dible flower gallery

Pick flowers that are fully open, but not ...d. Deadheading (cutting off) ...d flowers will encourage the ...ant to make new buds.

It takes about three months for the seeds ...o grow and flower.

Flowery treats

Our garden flowers don't just look good enough to eat—they really are! Wash them gently, then use them to make crunchy calendula cookies and a refreshing drink made from cucumber, lemon—and borage.

You will need:

For the calendula cookies

- 1¼ cups all-purpose flour, plus extra for dusting
- ⅓ cup confectioners' sugar
- grated zest of 1 orange
- 1 tbsp orange juice
- ½ cup salted butter, plus extra for greasing
- 1 egg yolk
- 4–8 calendula flowers, chopped

For the frosting

- ½ cup confectioners' sugar
- 1 tbsp orange juice
- 2–4 calendula flowers, chopped

For the borage refresher

- 1 medium cucumber
- 2½ cups cold water
- 2 lemons
- 2 tbsp superfine sugar
- 6–12 borage flowers

borage refresher

calendula cookies

Calendula cookies

These flower-shaped cookies are made with chopped calendula petals.

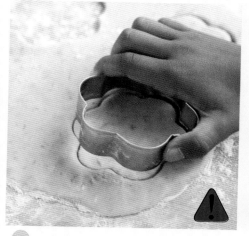

1 **Sift flour** and confectioners' sugar into a bowl. Add the orange zest, juice, butter, egg, and calendula. Beat to form a dough. Then wrap in plastic wrap and chill for 30 minutes.

2 **Preheat** the oven to 375°F (190°C). On a floured surface, roll out the dough to ⅛ in (3 mm) thick. Cut into flower shapes. Arrange on a greased baking sheet. Cook for 8–10 minutes, until golden.

3 **For the frosting,** beat the confectioners' sugar with the orange juice. When the cookies are cool, put a dollop of frosting in the middle of each one. Sprinkle with chopped petals.

ice cubes

Borage refresher

Add borage flowers to a summer drink or use to make ice cubes.

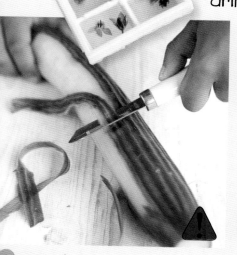

3 **Squeeze the** lemons. Put the juice in a pitcher, along with the cucumber liquid, sugar, and borage flowers. Chill before serving.

1 **Peel the cucumber,** then cut the flesh into rough chunks. Puree in a food processor with the cold water.

2 **Strain the pulp,** pushing it through the strainer with the back of a spoon.

Growing wheat

You would need a very big field to grow enough wheat to provide your family with bread for a year. However, one crateful should make enough flour for a small but delicious, cakelike tea loaf. You won't need a combine harvester, either!

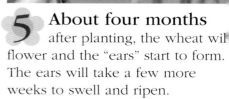

Important stuff

Grow wheat in an open area that gets sunshine all day.

Keep the compost lightly moi̇ but do not overwater. Chec̟ the compost before wateri̇

Plant seeds in the spring and harvest i̇ the fall.

Some varieties of wheat can be planted in the fall for harvest the next summer.

Plant a windmill or plastic flags in your wheat to keep the birds off your crop!

1 **Line an old** wooden crate or similar container with a piece of black plastic. Make holes in the bottom for drainage. Fill the box with all-purpose compost and rake it flat.

2 **Thinly sow the wheat** seeds on the surface. Aim for roughly one grain every 1 in (2.5 cm). Lightly cover the grain with more compost, and water the seeds.

3 **After two weeks,** the first shoots should start to appear. Grasses, such as wheat, produce only a single seed leaf. If any weeds start to grow, pull them out.

4 **Water the wheat** regularly in dry weather but don't get it too wet. The first real leaves should start to appear after four weeks.

5 **About four months** after planting, the wheat wil̇ flower and the "ears" start to form. The ears will take a few more weeks to swell and ripen.

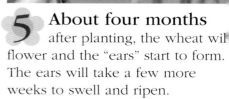

6 **When the wheat** starts to change color you know it is nearly ready to harvest. It will turn a golden color and the ears will bend over. Check for ripeness by biting on a grain. If it is hard, the grain is ready. If it is soft, leave it a little longer.

7 **Cut the wheat at the** base of the stem. Tie it into bundles and stand it upright. Leave it in a sunny but sheltered place for a few weeks to dry out and finish ripening.

Threshing and milling

Once your wheat has dried out, the grains can be turned into flour. First, you need to separate the grains from the stalks. This process is called threshing. Then you can mill (grind) the grains.

There can be as many as 50 grains in an ear of wheat. Each one is a seed.

1 Put the wheat into an old pillowcase with the ears at one end and the stalks sticking out of the other.

2 Now for the fun part. Hold the open end of the pillowcase tightly around the stalks and bash the wheat against a wall. The wheat grains separate from the stalks and fall to the bottom of the pillowcase.

3 **Pour the grain** and pieces of debris called chaff into a bowl. Grain is heavier than chaff, so you can separate it by pouring it from one container to another in a light breeze. The grain falls into the container and the chaff blows away. This is called winnowing.

grain

chaff

4 **To grind the wheat** into flour, use a coffee grinder. Pour the grains in the top, put the lid on, and turn it on. The grains quickly turn to flour. Pour this out and repeat.

coffee grinder

wheat grains

milled flour

Science stuff

What's inside a seed?

The outside is called the husk. Millers call it BRAN and it is full of fiber, vitamins, and minerals, which our bodies need to stay healthy.

The inside is called the ENDOSPERM. This is a mixture of starches and proteins that provides the seed with energy to grow. It is used to make white flour.

The germ is where the seed starts to grow (germinate). It contains proteins and oils. Whole-wheat flour uses the GERM, BRAN, and ENDOSPERM.

Whole-wheat tea loaf

Whole-wheat flour is an essential ingredient in this fruity, cakelike tea loaf. It's super easy to make, and is best eaten while still warm from the oven—either plain, or spread with creamy butter.

You will need:

- butter, for greasing
- 1/2 cup dried mixed fruit (raisins, golden raisins, currants)
- 1/2 cup dried cranberries
- 3 1/2 fl oz (100 ml) warm tea
- 2 tbsp honey
- 1 egg, beaten
- 1 1/4 cups whole-wheat flour
- 1 tbsp baking powder
- 1/2 tsp apple-pie spice

1 Preheat the oven to 350°F (180°C), then lightly grease a 1 lb (450 g) loaf pan with butter. Pour the dried mixed fruit and cranberries into a bowl.

2 Pour the warm tea over the fruit and stir everything together.

3 Then add the honey and beaten egg and gently mix together.

4 Add the whole-wheat flour, baking powder, and apple-pie spice. Stir well to combine all the ingredients.

5 Spoon the mixture into the prepared pan and level the top. Bake for 20–25 minutes, or until cooked through.

Top tip

Is the tea loaf cooked? To find out, push a skewer into the middle. Then pull it out. If it comes out clean, the tea loaf is ready.

Plants for watery places

If you live in a climate where it's cloudy or rains a lot, it's a good idea to choose plants for your garden that like it damp and that thrive in moist soil and some shade.

Rhubarb

The bigger the better

Wet-weather winners tend to have large, lush green leaves. These jumbo leaves are great for catching water and directing it down the stem toward the roots. They protect the soil, too, stopping it from drying out too quickly. In cloudy conditions, they also expose the maximum surface of the plant to the sun to help the plant make its own food.

Iris

Flag irises are spring-flowering plants that love damp or waterlogged places. They are often found at the edges of ponds and rivers.

Hostas come in a fabulous range of leaf colors and sizes. Give them some shade and keep them well watered and they will treat you to a wonderful display.

Look after your **primulas**, since they don't like to be too hot or cold, or too soggy. If they like where you are growing them, you will be able to divide the clump every few years, increasing your supply of a beautiful flowering plant.

Hosta

Primula

...unnera looks like ...nt rhubarb. There ...e more than 40 ...ecies, some of ...ich are used as ...od or medicine.

Giant gunnera

is a huge plant—just one leaf can reach 5 ft (1.5 m) across! It is only suitable for large gardens and grows well in a bog area or the edge of a pond. If you visit a garden where giant gunnera is growing, be careful—it has spiked prickles under its leaves.

Growing rhubarb

Rhubarb is not actually a fruit—it's a vegetable, and it's very easy to grow. The plants need hardly any care—they'll grow and ripen almost by themselves. Just make sure you give them plenty of water, so they produce lovely juicy stems.

Important stuff

Rhubarb grows best in a sunny position or partial shade.

The plants need lots of moisture in summer, so water them regularly.

Don't cut any stems during the first growing season, so the roots have time to mature.

To pick your rhubarb, hold each stalk close to the base, then twist it out. This encourages more stems to grow in its place.

seeds

crown

one-year-old plant

There are three ways to grow rhubarb—from seeds, from a crown (root cutting), and from a small plant. We're starting with a small plant.

1 **Little rhubarb plants** are sold in nurseries and garden centers. They are best planted in late fall.

2 **Choose a container** that's about 2 ft (60 cm) across. Ask an adult to make drainage holes in the bottom.

3 **Plant the rhubarb** plant in all-purpose compost. Make sure the top of the root is around 1 in (2.5 cm) below the surface.

4 **Rhubarb** is a big plant, so give it plenty of space. The leaves will die down in the winter and sprout again in the spring.

5 **When your rhubarb** plant begins to grow again, cover it with a bucket or laundry basket to keep out the light. Lift the cover regularly to water the rhubarb.

If the plant is shaded from the sun it cannot make green chlorophyll, which is why the stems stay pink.

6 **Keeping rhubarb** in the dark encourages the stalks to stay pinkish red and taste sweet. This process is called "forcing."

Plant watch

Forcing rhubarb should only be done every other year, and then for only eight weeks early in the season.

If the temperature gets very cold, try wrapping straw around the pot to keep the plant warm.

Top tip

Never eat rhubarb leaves—they're highly poisonous!

75

Rhubarb cobblers

A cobbler is a baked fruit dessert with a topping that resembles a biscuit or a dumpling. Often, it's made in one large dish, but this recipe is for four individual cobblers.

You will need:

- 12 oz (350 g) rhubarb, cut into 3/4 in (2 cm) pieces
- grated zest of 1 orange
- 1/4 cup soft brown sugar
- 1 tbsp cornstarch
- 1½ cups self-rising flour
- 1/4 cup butter, cut into cubes
- 1/4 cup superfine sugar, plus extra for sprinkling
- ½ cup milk, plus extra for brushing

1 **Put the rhubarb,** orange zest, sugar, and cornstarch in a bowl and stir together. Let the fruit sit for 10–15 minutes.

2 **Meanwhile,** make the topping: put the flour in a large bowl, then add the butter. Use your fingertips to rub the butter into the flour until the mixture looks like fine bread crumbs.

3 **Stir in the sugar,** then add the milk a little at a time until you have a slightly sticky, soft dough.

4 **Transfer the dough** to a lightly floured surface and pat it out until it's ½ in (1 cm) thick. Cut the dough into 8 rounds.

5 **Divide the rhubarb** between 4 ovenproof dishes. Put 2 biscuits on top of each. Brush with milk and sprinkle with sugar.

Cook it

Preheat the oven to 350°F (180°C). Put the cobblers on a baking sheet and bake for 25–30 minutes, until the topping is golden.

Try serving this dish with ice cream or custard.

Glossary

Aquatic plant A plant whose roots are permanently under water. The rest of the plant may also be fully submerged or float on the surface.

Carnivorous plant A plant that captures and eats insects to obtain nutrients that it cannot get from the soil.

Chlorophyll The green pigment found in plant leaves and stems that is used by the plant to convert the Sun's energy into food.

Compost Potting compost is a special soil mix for growing plants in pots. Garden compost is a soil improver made from decayed plants.

Cuttings Method of making new plants by taking pieces of plant stem and encouraging them to grow new roots.

Fertilizer A mixture of nutrients that encourages plants to grow.

Flower This is the structure that contains the male and female parts of the plant.

Forcing Method of encouraging plants to make early growth.

Fruit The part of a plant that develops from the ovary at the base of a flower. Many fruits have a fleshy outer case that protects the seeds.

Germination When seeds begin to grow by sending out their first root and shoot.

Grasses A family of flowering plants that have narrow leaves growing from the base. They include the cereal crops, such as wheat and barley.

Hilling up Building up soil around a potato plant's stem to encourage it to send out roots where new potatoes will grow.

Hybrid A new variety of plant that has resulted from two parent plants of different species.

Leaf One of the parts of a plant where photosynthesis occurs.

Nutrient A substance that is essential for plant growth.

Pesticide A chemical that is used to kill insects, slugs, snails, and other small creatures that damage plants.

Photosynthesis This is a process that takes place in a plant's leaves and stems. The leaves and stems take in carbon dioxide from the air and use sunlight to combine it with water from the soil to make food for the plant. Oxygen is a waste product of photosynthesis and is released into the air.

Pollination The process of transferring pollen from the male part of a flower to the female part so that seeds can be produced.

Roots The underground parts of a plant that take up nutrients and water from the soil and anchor the plant.

Seed The part of a flowering plant that contains a baby plant and a store of food to get it started.

Topiary Cutting trees and shrubs so that they grow into interesting shapes.

Vegetable The edible leaf, stem, or root of a plant. Some plants that are commonly called vegetables, such as bell peppers and tomatoes, are actually fruits.

Index

Acknowledgments

Dorling Kindersley would like to thank:

Capel Manor College
The Walled Garden, Gunnersbury Park,
Popes Lane, London W3 8LQ
for the use of its garden and
for taking care of our plants.

The Capel Manor Team
Tony Monaghan
Sarah Neophytou
Joanna Bates

Photographer
Will Heap
www.willheap.com

 **Secret Seed Society** creates vegetable adventures that will have children growing, eating, and talking about food in fun and healthy ways. It provided all the plant characters in this book.

You can find out more at www.secretseedsociety.com

A big thanks also to:

• Vauxhall City farm for use of its gardens for additional photography.

• RAGT Seeds for supplying wheat products.

• Meredith Mistry for making sweet-smelling lavender buddies.

• David Crawford for making corn paper.

• Jim Arbury, RHS Wisley, for supplying loofah plants.

• The staff at Shoots Garden Centre, Stanmore, Middlesex, for plants and advice.

• David Arnold, Sutton Seeds, for the supply of tomato, corn, and pepper plants.

• Jon Wheatley and Mary Payne MBE, horticultural consultant, Stonebarn Landscapes Limited, for the supply of vegetable plants.

• Hannah and Molly for illustrating the corn paper and notebooks on page 21.

Picture credits

The publisher would like to thank the following for their kind permission to reproduce their photographs:

(Key: a-above; b-below/bottom; c-center; f-far; l-left; r-right; t-top)

Alamy Images: Blickwinkel / Jagel 11crb; Rosemary Calvert 23cr; Martin Fowler 23ftr; Richard Heyes 31c; Dave Marsden 72-73b; Robert Harding Picture Library Ltd 63tr. **Chris Booth / monkeypuzzle:** 39tr. **Corbis:** AgStock Images 6b; Nigel Pavitt / JAI 11bl. **FLPA:** Tony Hamblin 23tr; Gary K. Smith 23tl. **Getty Images:** Digital Vision / VisionsofAmerica / Joe Sohm 10tr; Image Source 63ftr; The Image Bank / Jetta Productions 22-23b; The Image Bank / Simon Russell 11tl; The Image Bank / Ted Russell 22-23; iStock Exclusive / Aimin Tang 23ftl; Photodisc / Fromer 14tr, 20tr, 24tr, 26cla, 28cl, 32cl, 36tr, 40cla, 46cla, 50l, 56cla, 58cl, 60cla, 64bl, 64cla, 70cl, 75crb, 76cl, 77bl; Photodisc / Michael Grimm 63ftl; Photodisc / Steve Wisbauer 10cl; Photographer's Choice / Kevin Summers 22fclb; Photographer's Choice / Lester Lefkowitz 10bl; Veer Rogovin 10c. **iStockphoto. com:** Ana Faerman 10cr; FlamingPumpkin 10cra; Nikolay Postnikov 11ca. **Luigi FDV:** 23c. **Joy Michaud / Sea Spring Photos:** 35fcr; **Photolibrary:** Leroy Alfonse 4-5; imagebroker 73. **Steven Moore Photography:** 2bl, 2fbr, 3ftl, 34ca, 35cr, 50tr, 80cla, 80fcla. **Barbara Walton:** 63tc.

All other images © Dorling Kindersley
For further information see: www.dkimages.com

 Thank you everyone

Our models

Here are some of the lovely models who took part in the photos.

Cherry Camron Sophia Zeynep Christian Hannah Solly
Thanks also to Fiona and Molly for additional modeling.